CH00829636

Mirrors of Eternity

Reflections of the Soul

Ashian Belsey

Pen Press Publishers
London

Mirrors of Eternity

Reflections of the Soul

Ashian Belsey

First Published in Great Britain by
Pen Press Publishers Ltd
39-41 North Road
Islington
London
N7 9DP

ISBN 1 900796 29 5

A catalogue record for this book is available from the
British Library

Printed and bound in Great Britain
by Antony Rowe Ltd, Chippenham, Wiltshire

Cover design by
Remko Arentz

CONTENTS

ACKNOWLEDGEMENTS

To my partner Remko for coming into my life at just the right moment! For your perseverance, love, tolerance and gentleness – I thank you.

To Stuart Wilson and Kathryn Nicholls, thank you, dear friends, for your love, support and much needed help with spelling and grammar.

To Peter White, you are like a brother to me, thank you for being here.

To Sylvia Weston, thank you, dear friend, for your unconditional love and your belief in me.

To my dear wise dog Floyd, who lovingly has been my guardian and companion for the past ten years, thank you, dear soul.

To Pen Press for believing enough in my work – thank you all.

And last, but certainly not least, I wish to give a big thank you to all the ascended masters and the angelic host who have been my guides throughout this lifetime. I cherish the 'intense' moments that we've shared.

FOREWORD

Please note that our directness is brought to you with the utmost compassion. We respect and honour you more than you know, and because of this we will not treat you like children, for you have outgrown this position. Instead we will treat you as equals and as the divine souls that you truly are. We feel that as equals and because we do not wish to patronise you in any way, we can talk to you directly without 'treading softly', so as not to 'step on eggshells'. We trust in you, we know what you are capable of.

This is a very compact little book. We have chosen to make it so because we wish to focus only on what needs your attention at this time. We could give you many more subjects of interest but this would only take your attention away from what we wish to share with you, what we feel needs your immediate attention. We do not believe in using words for words' sake, just to make this book longer or perhaps more entertaining; it is not our job at this time to be the entertainers.

We know that you will take our love and our messages to your hearts. Directly in love, let us commence.'

The following information was gathered over the short period of two months. It has been a great privilege to work with such beautiful energies. For the great part of this book the 'voice' remains unknown. There did not seem the need to ask nor question the source. I hope this little book will help and inspire you to cut through some of life's illusions and fundamentally lead you further into the light.

INTRODUCTION

As I gaze out of the window at the snow-covered fields, I let my mind drift back over the last few years. It's incredible how so much has happened to completely change my life and the way I view it. In a sense, life can and will never be the same again.

I entered this world pretty much the same as anyone else, although I was born at our family home rather than at a hospital. My childhood was pretty dreary, I would say. I was very much a timid shy child who wouldn't say boo to a goose. I went through the rebellious years of the teens and left home at fifteen to 'find myself'. Boyfriends came and went until I fell head over heels for Pete. It was love at first sight and in my eyes he could do no wrong. We became engaged, much to the dismay of my parents, who could not stand the sight of him.

In 1979 the first of the changes began. Pete and I had been out one evening with friends at a local nightclub and on the way home we had a pretty serious car accident. Thankfully I don't remember too much about it, because I slipped into unconsciousness as we approached the wall. After the impact, the car flipped over onto its roof. I was in the back seat and flew out through the windscreen, landing on the road. The car landed on top of me.

I spent the next week unconscious in intensive care.

I had a fractured scull and the staff told my parents that I might not make it. A week later I limped out on a stick with an enormous black eye. I felt very distant from people. My parents became almost strangers and Pete, who I had loved with all my heart, got 'the big elbow'.

Life became very confusing and so I embarked on the drug scene. I became involved with a group of people who experimented with every drug they could get their hands on. To begin with it was fun and we travelled to various festivals, got as high as kites and then spent the next few days recovering.

This continued for a few years. I didn't notice as the fun aspect gradually disappeared, to be replaced by paranoia, fear and dependency. I remember going to the bathroom one morning after a 'heavy' party the night before and staring at three used needles lying in the bath tub. Something that morning shocked me so much that I got up and left, moving to a quiet sleepy little seaside town, where I promised myself I would never touch another drug again. I spent the next year releasing the drugs from my system and slowly began to feel 'normal'.

The next turn in events came in 1993. I had never been particularly interested in anything spiritual; about the nearest I had come to it was an occasional visit to a clairvoyant. However, something led me to attend a small meditation group. I began to enjoy the meetings and started to open my eyes to the possibility of other life forms. My third eye began to open, although I was often shown things that I couldn't properly interpret.

One day a friend arrived at my flat with some

cassettes. These tapes were to change my life totally. They were a set of channelled tapes about Ascension from Eric Klein. I sat and sobbed and sobbed as I listened to them. I now understand about the importance of words and how energy, keys and codes are held within them. The word 'Ascension' was my trigger. I wish to thank Eric for such beautiful work. I often wonder how many others it 'awoke'.

I have since noticed over the years how the word 'Ascension' can affect people. Some become quite angry and refuse to even mention it. For others, like myself, it's a doorway to a whole new world, one which I just wanted to explore as far as I could. As my curiosity grew, so did my abilities. I had visited a clairvoyant and he told me to buy a crystal and place it under my pillow for one night. This I did and the dreams that I had that night were so intense, it seemed like my whole life - or should I say lives - flashed before me.

The following evening I was sitting trying to watch a programme on TV but the crystal kept catching my eye. In the end I turned the TV off and picked up the crystal. It was so beautiful. The candles I had lit flickered, catching the rainbows within the crystal. I slowly closed my eyes, took a few deep breaths and relaxed. Just then I heard a voice. It was so close to my ear that I nearly jumped out of the chair in shock. However, the voice spoke in such a loving way that I couldn't be frightened. It is difficult to remember its exact words, for it all happened so quickly. I do remember being told that 'they' had been preparing me for some time and that 'they' wished to speak through me. The voice spoke a little longer as the tears rolled down my face; the energy was so intense and loving. I asked the speaker who he was and he replied that all I needed to know was that he was a Master from the Light and that I would get to know them all much better in the days to come. With that he left.

Needless to say, I was in shock afterwards. But a few cigarettes later I rang the lady who ran the meditation group. She asked me to go round to her home the following evening to try some channelling, and so my new life began.

Every Sunday afternoon I would drive to the meditation group. I was channelling beings such as Sananda, (Jesus) Kuthumi and Archangel Michael.

I was so thrilled to be given such a wonderful opportunity that channelling became not just part of my life but all of it! I would be 'chatting' to my new friends from the moment I awoke: driving the car, washing up, you name it, my friends were always there gently encouraging and teaching me. Although I had a lot of fun channelling, I took my new role very seriously, as some of the information that came through was often quite profound about the Earth and the changes that were taking place upon it.

As the weeks went by I noticed that some of my close friends in the group began to be increasingly jealous, and with this they became sceptical about my channellings. I didn't mind though, I wasn't lonely: how could I be? I would rush back from my work as a console operator, climb into bed and call in 'the gang'! The experiences I had of being lifted gently into their arms and held was breathtaking - sometimes literally! I would fall asleep safely in their embrace.

Months passed and I could feel an uneasiness

amongst the group because of these experiences I claimed to have. Nobody really said anything, but the doubting faces said it all. I was constantly being told by Sananda that something was going to occur in my life and that I should not be frightened. It was in June of that year that Sananda's words came back to me. I was at the meditation group one Sunday afternoon when I suddenly got such a strong aching in my shoulder that I asked Pete, a member of the group, if he would massage it for me. Pete's energies are amazing and as soon as he laid his hand on my shoulder, something strange began to happen. I felt as though I was about to pass out, the room started to spin, I felt nauseous and I was unable to focus on anyone in the room. Their voices seemed to be fading away. I muttered to Pete to get me into the garden. He carried me out and placed me on the grass; he later told me that I had become a deathly white colour and felt freezing to the touch.

I wasn't sure what to expect and although somewhat frightened, I knew I should give in to this strange process with trust. Feeling myself being lifted, almost as if I was in a hammock being slowly rocked, I began to feel quite nauseous. I also felt very emotional. I landed on a marble table, and was aware of a being standing at the end of this table. Although I wasn't looking directly at him, I knew it was Sananda. He started to speak to me. 'Look into my eyes,' he said. I said that I couldn't as it was too emotional. He repeated, 'Look into my eyes' and so, taking a deep breath, I turned my head and looked into the most incredible pair of eyes I have ever seen. The love that I felt was so pure that I burst into tears. He stretched out his arms and said, 'Are you ready to come with me?' I couldn't believe it - why me? I thought. I hesitated, out of fear, I suppose. Where would I be going? But a moment later, I replied, 'Yes, I'm ready.' He said, 'Do not worry, you will have another two experiences such as this and on the third you will come with me.' With this I was gently lowered back down.

By this time I had caused quite a commotion in the garden. The group could see me lying on the grass, muttering things under my breath about Sananda and crying my eyes out! Well, that did it! They really thought I'd flipped, but still I continued to attend their meetings.

Everyone avoided the subject of my experience, but I began to look forward to my next journey with Sananda. Then, as he had promised, the same process started to happen again when I was with the group. The room started to spin, so I asked if I could lie down. Somehow I managed to make it upstairs to one of the bedrooms and some members of the group followed me up, curious to see what would happen. Again I felt myself being lifted and feeling very sick. This time I went a bit further, and ended up in a black space. I felt totally alone, and because of this, fear crept back in. The fear brought me straight back down. I was disappointed in myself for not having the courage to go further, but was determined to try again.

In fact, that very evening I got another chance, this time lying downstairs in their front room. Some of the group were still there, and one of them said that he saw my etheric body sit up and walk out of my material body. Again I entered the dark area I now know is the 'void'. Once again I felt alone but, as the fear

6

crept in, I battled with it, desperately not wanting to miss my last opportunity to go on further. However, once again my fear stopped the process and, to my disappointment, I felt myself coming back down. On the way down I heard Sananda say that I wasn't to worry and that I would have one more attempt.

The weeks went by, and would you believe it, yes, I was at another group meeting when it began to happen all over again. We were sitting outside listening to some friends play the didgeridoo and singing. It was early evening and I suddenly began to feel very nauseous. The feeling seemed to intensify, so I got up and went inside the house, lying down on the floor. I knew what was happening and decided that the only way I was going to actually have the courage to go further was if I was at home in my bed and away from any disbelieving energies. Having made up my mind, I staggered out of the house. I still to this day do not recall the journey home, which incidentally was about five miles away; all I know is that I had some other help driving the car.

It was 9pm when I fell into bed. I called the masters to me and asked for Archangel Michael to help me. Though I was still very nervous as I didn't really know what was going to happen, I knew I had to find the courage to continue. After affirming I would like to try again, I was suddenly put into a deep, deep sleep. I say deep sleep but I was still aware of currents of energy travelling up and down my body, almost like electricity but not uncomfortable.

At midnight the masters awoke me, again in the void, only this time I wasn't frightened. I felt very alone but safe, almost as if I was in a very large womb. This lasted only a few moments and I was immediately given a large book. It was very old and thick and the pages were beginning to discolour with age. I asked what I should do with this book, and was told just to observe.

With that the pages flicked over; the pictures seemed to be telling a story. As quickly as the book arrived it vanished and a baby appeared. It was in a sort of tunnel and although I wasn't told, I knew what to do. With my mind I made the baby travel along the tunnel until it came out of the end into an ocean. As it came to the surface it took a gasp of air and so did I. The baby then vanished and was replaced by a door which was surrounded by a golden glow. As I neared it, the door was opened by a man with dark hair and brown eyes, wearing a long white robe. He looked similar to Sananda; whoever he was, I seemed to know him. Smiling, he welcomed me in.

I walked through into a large golden room with a wooden floor and very large portraits on the walls. I noticed that there were no windows in the room, just small wooden chairs all the way around the edge. I was guided up to the end of the room where there was a large wooden table, and there I was greeted by Sananda, who stood behind it. We shook hands and he said, 'Congratulations!' I remember saying something like 'If I knew it was going to be this easy I would never have been scared', and he smiled lovingly. It's funny because I loved Sananda so much, almost idolising him, and yet at that moment I was greeting him as an equal and an old friend. He then said he would erase the rest of the conversation from my mind but he would trigger me as I went through life. With that, I was suddenly back in my bed.

Dazed, I looked about my bedroom and at the clock, which read 2am. But what year? And what date? How long had I been gone? I felt strange and confused. Slowly I got out of bed and walked along the dark corridor to the bathroom. As I turned on the light I caught a glimpse of myself in the mirror and what a shock I got! It was my face, but with clear blue eyes and skin that seemed to radiate light. Shocked, I quickly got back into bed. My body felt different, sort of light and floaty.

After a few minutes I got back out of bed and was about to get into my car to drive over to some friends when I was 'advised' not to as I would blow the fuses in the car. I remember thinking to myself that I knew everything there was to know about anything. I tried to make a cup of tea but couldn't remember how to. Instead I thought that perhaps a hot bath would help ground me. I walked over to the boiler to feel if the water was hot enough; it was cold but as I felt the boiler it suddenly began to get hot!

Feeling shocked, I decided to go back to bed. I awoke mid-morning and felt more or less 'back to normal'. A little later I returned to the group and told them of my experiences. They didn't believe me and I felt very alone and hurt, and as the weeks went by I slowly isolated myself from them.

Life carried on, although it was becoming increasingly difficult for me to remain at work, I just didn't feel that I belonged there any more. I was advised by Sananda to give up my work and to trust that I would be sent people for healing and readings; he also told me not to advertise. Well, that was a test of faith, as I was earning good money at the garage,

9

but I went ahead and handed in my notice. That week at work another strange thing happened.

I was at the garage when all of a sudden the road became absolutely still, there wasn't a car to be seen. There was a strange atmosphere, it was too quiet! A car, the same model as my own, drove in. A young girl got out and put in some petrol, and for some reason I couldn't take my eyes off her. She had long blond hair tied in a pony tail, and very clear blue eyes. We seemed so similar that it was almost like looking at myself! She walked in and up to the counter to pay; she didn't say a word, just smiled at me, a sort of knowing smile, handed me the money and was gone. I was left shaking and had to go into the back room to calm down. She affected me so much that I could have easily sobbed and sobbed.

I now know that I was visited by an Angel.

After this I spent one and a half years of intense 'going within', under the watchful eye of Sananda and El Morya. They told me to try and master 'every aspect of self'. I had to try and address every issue that is in this book. At times Sananda would appear in front of me and gently talk to me for hours. These were very special times for me and times that I still hold dearly in my heart.

At times they led me gently and at other times very firmly until one day they 'disappeared' from my energy field. I questioned why they had left me so abruptly. 'We have not left you, child, it is just that we no longer walk in front of you but by your side,' they said. 'Congratulations! It is now time to start working with your I Am Presence, your own source of information.'

In March 1998, the day before my 34th birthday, I

was given the opportunity to leave the earth plane and work from other levels.

I hadn't been feeling well for a few weeks but had put it down to a flu virus that had been going around the village. One morning I awoke feeling a little better and so I decided to go out for some fresh air. I was walking along a lane when I very clearly heard a voice saying, 'Your mission on earth is up for completion, you will have the choice whether to stay or come with us.'

The voice vanished, leaving me in a state of shock and disbelief. 'My mission is up for completion?' I questioned. 'But I haven't done anything yet!' I went back home and one hour later I found myself collapsing from intense pain onto the floor where I stayed for the following five hours. Eventually I managed to reach the phone and somehow managed to call a dear friend who rang for an ambulance. I arrived at the hospital with half an hour to live (according to the surgeon). There they told me I had a ruptured ectopic pregnancy and I had to have one of my tubes removed. I received a good deal of blood.

Throughout the experience I was in the loving presence of some beautiful beings who at the time seemed familiar. They again asked me if I wished to stay or go with them; needless to say I chose to stay. They visited me again a few weeks later at home in the middle of the night. They came to connect me to a 'higher part of self'. I haven't seen them since nor have I seen the ascended masters I grew so fond of. At times they will 'sweep in' with words of encouragement and love, but for the most part I now work only with my I Am Presence.

11

I feel very thankful to my teachers. My path wasn't and still isn't altogether an easy path. I seemed to have chosen a very intense and focused path for myself. I acknowledge that everyone's path is different and what is right for one is not necessarily right for another. I hope that you will enjoy your visit to the earth plane, learn what you can and take that valuable experience back with you, to wherever that may be!

In joy,
Ashian

MOTHER GAIA

I am Gaia, Mother Earth, and I greet you in love and peace. Do not underestimate me, for I am a very powerful being and I know exactly what I am doing. I tell you now that I do not need 'saving' for I know of my connection to All That Is. I say to you all with the deepest of love, the love that a mother has for her children, to first heal yourselves. Only in this way will you assist me with my healing process.

In truth this is all that you need to do: heal thy self. When all are healed within, all will heal 'outside' of self for life is a mirroring process.

'I am whole and I ask you to become whole too. In love I am.'

During this enlightening experience, I was taken down a vortex and held suspended at the bottom, held in a loving energy while Mother Gaia spoke to me with such love but also such strength. Usually I am taken upwards and suspended at the top of a vortex where certain beings will either just talk to me for a while or sometimes appear in front of me to teach me.

At times I have been walking my lovely old dog and have felt slightly dizzy, so I have stopped and leaned against something to steady myself and then been given some information. Usually it is personal information, but sometimes information to be shared. The

13

information in this book came to me via a number of beings of the light. They have stated that it is not important to give names, but more important to feel their energies, love and support as you read these words.

CHAPTER 1

THE GREAT DIVIDE

Reflection:
'Internal conflict is the root to separation'

Greetings, friends, let us surround you in a blanket of energy while you read. It is with great joy that we take this opportunity to reach you like this. Bless you.

The more your planet moves into light the more those in fear will move into the darkness and confusion of their fear. Do not turn a blind eye to those in fear, but do not be pulled in by your quest to 'save' them. Offer supportive help to these souls if asked of you, but do not stay behind in a mission of mercy that is illusory.

You have had many years to prepare yourselves for these times. There are no excuses, you have the tools. We told you to prepare yourselves for the changes to come and those changes are upon you now. The time you have waited for is here. There is not the time left to prepare further - come as you are, ready or not.

We have led you on a long and weary path. Like the prodigal son we let you explore the deepest and

15

darkest jungles of your beingness. You had plenty of preparation and time to work on your fear issues and to heal them. We led you out the other side of your inner jungle and into your tower of oneness. A great deal of you have made it out the other side, perhaps feeling a little battered and bruised from your experiences, but nevertheless you've done it! And we congratulate you, for it is a big achievement. Some of you are still trying to find your way out and you will be helped. We say this to you with great compassion.

For those who remain within the jungle of their own fears and continue to create their own monsters, there will be a scenario that will be seen to take place. You have heard before of the scenario of two people standing together on a street and both experiencing different things? Well, this will be the case. Those persons standing next to you living in fear will see only fear wherever they look. They will live it, see it and dream it. All their friends and neighbours will live it, it will be their reality and only fear will be attracted to these people.

Likewise, those that step more into the light, focusing only on light, will experience only light. Fear will not be their reality. Do not 'buy into' fear. See all the dramas taking place, but turn quietly to the light. Leave behind you a trail of light for others to follow but do not leave your whole self.

Avoid any literature that feeds fear, for there will be much, it will come in disguise, claiming to inform you, but in truth it will lead you away from truth; for truth is always without fear. Truth uplifts the spirit, helping it to grow. It never leaves you feeling uneasy in any way. If you come across any such material in your future, we would advise that you put it calmly to one side. Do not give it any energy by thinking about it in any way. In fact it is not worth discussing it with anyone for if you do, you are unknowingly adding energy to it.

Recently there has been a war that threw many people into fear and confusion [Kosovo]. Try to look at this from a higher perspective and see what is taking place. See with a higher vision if you will. From a lower perspective it will appear to be very destructive and very fearful, it will seem as if many 'poor souls' are suffering at the mercy of evil.

If you take that reality to a higher level and look again you will see the necessity of this war. The area in which this war took place has many dense 'stuck' energy patterns. The only way to release these patterns is to literally blow them to the surface to transmute and transform to higher and finer energy. We do not wish to sound harsh when we say to you that the 'poor souls suffering the evil' agreed on a higher level to assist in raising man's consciousness through the compassion that is stirred within people. From our perspective the plan worked wonderfully. These beautiful souls' work succeeded. They were not destroyed by evil, for in truth there is no evil, only a lower state of consciousness. The unity that this war brought about is quite beautiful to behold.

I would ask you to see through our eyes and to see the light in the situation, not the darkness. As we look at your planet we see enormous amounts of energy circling each and every one of you. This energy is so transforming that at times it can appear to be destructive, particularly to those still carrying fear within their matrix. As the intensity grows it will break down

17

all resistance in the body which will sometimes seem to produce illness, over-tiredness, aching of the body etc. We would urge you to continue to work upon yourselves through these times, helping to make the body stronger and more energised to help the process. Some are under the illusion of false thinking, believing that they can sit back and relax, paying no attention to the body and its needs. We observe that there is some lethargy, a belief system that some are able to transmute anything. Some can on the earth plane, but not many. There are not that many who are pure enough in their love to transmute anything. If they were, then nothing would be able to affect them. There can be a danger in believing you are further along the path than you actually are: this can make you lazy, which in turn pulls you into the illusory world. Keep sharp, my friends. Keep your wits about you! Continue to practise what you have been taught.

The energy will steadily increase over the next few years and at times you will feel as if you are on a roller-coaster without breaks! And, in a sense, you are! This is why it is so important to stay focused, live in the now, and try to stay out of fear, because if you can't handle it now, then it will be very difficult to handle it later on.

Remember that darkness is uninformed, it is low-level consciousness. Consciousness could be likened to several layers and levels within you and at the lowest level it is linked with darkness, ignorance, fear, jealousy, greed and all things associated with darkness. As you move up through the levels of consciousness you ascend more and more into light which is knowledge, love, truth and enlightenment. Eventually, if we can continue with our analogy, you will ascend to the top level which represents God or Source. When you reach this level of consciousness you will fully understand and know deep within your beingness that there is no separation in anything. There is no yin and yang, no form of judgement can reside there, no light or dark, no good or bad; there just 'is'. Only when you come back down through the levels of consciousness does separation occur. The mind takes over from the heart and analyses everything, trying to work everything out rationally and put everything into neat little packages. As you begin to *really* understand this concept you will understand why there is no need to fear 'evil', for it does not exist, at least not as it is portrayed; it is simply lower level consciousness. The light is always stronger for it is informed. With this in mind, go forward without fear, dear friends, enjoying your life.

We have touched on fear in the very first chapter: we do so to emphasise the importance of ending fear within your lives. We will be discussing fear many more times throughout these pages, to help lead you gently out of fear and further into the light. We choose to return to subjects simply because if we were to give you the whole of the information in one go it would 'overload' you and you would lose concentration. We are here to gently 'prod' at you, to help and assist you: to do so at such an important time requires a firm hand! We will not 'mollycoddle' you. We will, if you allow, help you to advance beyond your comprehension.

Eventually planet earth will be an ascended planet and so all who remain upon her will live in an ascended civilisation. However, this does not mean that you all instantly become masters of your own reality. This takes time and a lot of dedication. Ascension means one has ascended to higher levels of consciousness. The title 'master' means that one would have mastered the limitations of self in that dimension and would have mastered their lower self. Many will not have mastered all there is to master on the earth plane and will continue to strive for mastery in the new reality, providing that they manage to reach the higher levels of consciousness to be able to stay physically on the earth plane. Those who do not make the transition will depart for a new reality and one that is in harmony to their vibration. We have discussed fear, well many in fear will depart in fear. Choices are being made and 'new homes' are being prepared. Those in light will start to move further into the light, attracting only light to them. Those in fear [which is darkness, uninformed, without love] will attract like-minded people and events to them. This energy, as it draws together, can cause some pretty detrimental things to occur and so large amounts of people will move on in this way.

Some light helpers who have finished their work and personal growth upon the earth are also departing around this time, although there is always the choice to remain in service on earth. However, some will leave, as they will be called to work in other ways and perhaps, surprisingly, they will be able to return once the planet has made her ascension and there is a calmness present. There will be a settling in process. This will be a wondrous time and much rejoicing will take place. Many stories will be told. Groups of people will live together in harmony with the land and with each other. Foods will be grown from the freshened soil. There will be a new light to breathe, much finer, cleansed. Each of you have your own personal gifts and although many new psychic abilities will emerge, you will honour each other's abilities and work together in unity. There will not be the jealousy that exists with some of you now, there will be a feeling of love and an honouring of each other.

Large geometric buildings will be built on power lines which will be your 'hospitals,' although we prefer to call them houses of healing. 'Nurses' will be chosen for their role by their compassion and therefore their ability to heal. Colour therapy will be a very active source of healing. Colours will be beamed to the patient while sound is invoked, for sound is very important to the harmonising of one's energy fields and will be used widely.

The buildings that are currently used as churches will remain, although they will be somewhat revamped! They will not be used for power or for religious purposes as they are now, instead they will be 'great houses of wisdom' and places where people will gather regularly while certain speakers will inform the people and impart great wisdom and knowledge.

As people draw together in love there will emerge a great 'doorway of light.' Thus, my friends, a new dawn will commence.

We hope you have enjoyed the vision that we have just given you. One day it will become more than just a vision, it will become your reality.

Chapter 2

Planetary Vortexes and Parallel Realities

Reflection:
'Doors within doors, worlds within worlds.'

Your vibration is being raised. The more love and light you carry and express in your life, the higher your vibrational frequency will become. There are many, many vortexes upon your world, but for many people they will go unnoticed until their vibrations match that of the vortex. This is to safeguard your world against planetary invasion. The more you begin to work in harmony with your planet, the more you will be aware of these vortexes and will be conscious of travelling through them and into a new parallel reality.

If you are clairvoyant you will be able to see them and if you look at the colour that emits from them you will know what to expect in that reality. For example, there are many vortexes that are green, as that particular reality is undergoing healing. Perhaps you may have noticed, at times, while driving in your car, an energy change and a difference in the consciousness of the people living in that area. There is a good chance that you have just passed through a vortex. Perhaps you have heard us talk before in other texts about parallel realities and understood that there can be many different scenarios taking place in the same time-frame, overlapping time, as it were. There are indeed many realities simultaneously taking place, layer over layer.

Man has often looked to the stars and the other planets in your solar system and looked for other life signs, only to be disappointed. This is not because there are no other life forms, of course, but because he looks to them with third-dimensional vision and of course sees only a lifeless planet. If, however, he were able to access the 'time vortex' of the planet concerned then he would see a vast and thriving community.

Your eyes are being adjusted. This is all part of your changing body. There is no need to be alarmed if from time to time you feel as if a veil has been swept aside, unveiling briefly a new parallel reality, perhaps of a 'time gone by', where you are suddenly faced with what you call 'ghosts'! You may also experience the ascended realms and as your vibrations are raising higher and nearer to theirs, it will become much easier to communicate with such beings.

People will begin to 'time jump' more and more using these vortexes. Some of you will notice your vehicles reacting to the change of energies when passing through vortexes. Do not be surprised if they break down on the other side! There is often a noticeable difference in health matters. A person could experience illness in one reality and not in another, for the illness may not exist outside of that reality. If the illness wasn't born in that reality, your body may not recognise it. Perhaps having the awareness of such existing realities will enable you to take some necessary steps to look after your energy levels.

We have been discussing different realities, dimensions and levels. We would also like to help you become aware that there are also different 'levels' of answers and information given to you. We are giving you information from one level so that you can understand us on your level of understanding and in that level the information we give to you is truth. As you proceed along your 'self-illuminating' pathway of life you will be given further information coming from another level, higher in vibration, and you will become more informed. Think back to information given to you a year ago. See how it has changed, evolved and grown into something very new. Some of you have felt that you were deceived and misguided, for the information changed so quickly. We tell you now that you were not misguided, dear friends. You were not ready to receive the level of information that comes to you now.

As your planet evolves into a fourth and even fifth dimensional planet, dimensions begin to overlap one another which could make life a little confusing for a while. Objects may appear briefly then disappear again. 'Hidden mysteries' will be revealed, clues to your background will be uncovered shaking the belief systems of many.

As worlds overlap collapsing time, your memory may fade. This is not a process to worry about, dear friends, you will only remember that which really holds any importance; what is irrelevant will go.

You will begin to consciously walk with your brothers and sisters in outer worlds. Books like this will not be so needed for you will be able to communicate directly with us and many other dear souls. We look forward to these times with great anticipation and love in our hearts.

We have been patient, we long to embrace each and every one of you. We have watched you from our world and eagerly await your evolvement. We await you, our brothers and sisters, with our arms outstretched.

Chapter 3

Making Progress

Reflection:
'Any progress made within will reflect outward.'

We ask you to heal yourselves in order to heal the planet. We understand that for some this would seem like an enormous task. 'Where do we begin?' you may ask. We say to you to begin bit by bit, little by little, slowly beginning to heal the past. By healing the past you will begin to change the pattern of your life. Change your life for the better working little by little, slowly taking steps to improve your life in the way you would wish. We note that there are feelings of impatience in many, a desire to have everything *now* and have the 'end result' as quickly as possible. Learn to work more with patience and love. This way the results will come about far quicker, for only the energy of love has any power to it and therefore has the power to change situations. Frustration was never born from love.

One step at a time, we cannot emphasise this enough. Many experiences and valuable lessons will be learnt, creating more knowledge. Imagine, if you will, that you are handed a big box of your favourite chocolates. You may be tempted to eat them all at once, emptying the box quickly of its contents. You would then be left with an empty box and not remember a great deal about the taste of each individual chocolate - the experience might be lost. We urge you to take your time in 'eating your chocolates': savour the taste of each, experience fully each encounter.

Some on the earth plane find themselves in desperate situations and cannot see a way out. Again we would say to take one step at a time in the right direction. Always try and bring love into the situation, even in times of despair, for love has the ability to bring about change. Hardships are just illusions. Only that of love is truth and reality.

Remember that you are the centre of your own Universe. You will never heal outside of self first. Always begin slowly within. Do not be tempted, out of impatience, to try and release too much too quickly or else you may send your body into shock. Be gentle and loving with yourselves.

You may have noticed some strange occurrences with your weather patterns, have you not? Well, congratulations dear friends, many of you are doing very well with the self-healing process. You can see the mirroring effect of this process reflecting outside of self. There are many earthquakes, which shake free old patterning, downpours of torrential water, just like your emotions that pour from you in the form of tears. In fact water levels are rising. So are the amount of tears that are being shed by those going through their healing process. There are wild and sudden storms, just like the anger that you have been releasing. Do not fear your changing weather patterns for they signal a grand healing is taking place on a very large scale. Soon enough, calm and peaceful times will reign as the healing process within is over.

The earth is very good at transmitting dense, heavy energy, for she has a big heart overflowing with love and compassion. This is a very powerful tool for transmitting. Remember, darkness cannot live where there is love. Learn to love yourselves, though not from a sense of false pride, for this is ego and not true love. We speak of unconditional love, something many find very difficult. You may feel that you know all about unconditional love, but we know that you cannot, for we observe you looking at yourselves in your mirrors each day, criticising yourselves!

Begin within: you will never be able to love others unconditionally until you have the ability to love yourselves exactly as you are.

There is a constant searching, searching, searching to find self. My friends, you have already found self. You were never lost, that is an illusion. Many still take themselves off in solitude to find self. If you only knew that in fact you would 'find self' a lot quicker through being with others, observing and learning from them. Do you not know that you grow through love? Do not segregate yourselves. Have loving relationships and grow together in love. Many have taught that it is 'unspiritual' to have a relationship and have separated from marriages and relationships to walk their path alone.

We acknowledge that there are times when it is advisable to have time to oneself but you were never destined to be solitary beings, and by doing so, you are once again walking straight back into the separation that we have spoken of. Grow in love, dear ones. Grow and learn from each other, enjoy each other's companionship.

Drugs and drink will only lead you further from self, for they close down your gateway to your soul. So much so that only a 'shell' remains running on automatic pilot, breathing, talking and going through the motions of daily life, but without true quality of life. Do not be fooled into believing that drugs of any form will help you to grow quicker, for indeed this is an illusion.

You can never be a master of your reality, you are not in control, the habit is. The habit is the master, not you . This includes any form of habit from drugs to drink, smoking, nail-biting etc. Master your addictions, be in control.

You cannot buy self-esteem. Many of you have low self-worth and these issues need your attention. Why do you have such feelings of unworthiness? What is the root cause of these emotions? You need to go to the root of the 'problem' so that you can heal these feelings. Some of you, we notice, feel that it would all be better if you had plenty of money. Money would somehow make you feel so much better about yourself. Well, maybe so, or at least temporarily so. Once again, we repeat, you will never find happiness from an external source. You cannot hide behind money or any other crutch, sooner or later you will need to address these issues. You may as well make it sooner and save all the heartache.

Many still continue to ask what their role on earth is. Apart from the odd individual who has a very specific task to do, the rest of the light force can liken their work to that of the one named Jesus. You have the ability to do all the things that he did, maybe not yet to the extent that he did, but certainly enough to make a difference. Know that you are all the healer, the counsellor, the one that can 'calm the storm' and the one that leads many into the light. Oh, and don't forget to also be the child at times! Allow yourselves time to play and have fun. Many of you have become very serious, too serious.

It is one thing to be focused and another to be serious - lighten up! Laughter helps to raise the vibration of fear to a level where it cannot exist, so keep your sense of humour.

The more progress you make dealing with your 'internal stuff', the deeper into self you will go. Going deeper will not necessarily make life blissful. To always live in a state of bliss is illusory. The more 'whole' that you become the more you become 'whole' with All That Is.

Becoming one with All That Is can be both painful and blissful, for you become one with the emotions and anxieties of others, 'picking up' on others' feelings and thought patterns.

Beloveds, look into any master's eyes and you will see not only the joy but also the sadness within them. A great deal of progress is made for humanity by the transmuting of pain and sorrow by these beings.

We spoke of thought patterns. Understand that thoughts 'just are' and therefore do not belong to anyone. They are in a sense plucked out of the air by an individual and made that individual's own. When you have thoughts that are less than enlightening, do not become cross with yourselves for having such thoughts and dreams. Send love to these thoughts and send them on their way transformed. Know that it was just a thought that dropped into your consciousness; you do not need to make it yours.

Understand that you are not your thoughts and you are not your emotions. You are far more than you realise. Make progress slowly, steadily putting one foot in front of the other to ensure firm ground. That way you will not trip yourself up so much.

CHAPTER 4

DIARY OF ENLIGHTENMENT

Reflection:
'The tortoise and the hare.'

We have a new speaker for you this day and so we will step aside to allow his energies to mingle with the channel. Sit quietly for a moment or two while he adjusts his energy to match.

Good day, beloveds, I am Tai Ling. It is good to talk with you, is it not? I feel expanded in love and appreciation for you all. I will be new to many of you for I am a very quiet being who normally does not give speeches of any kind! However, I feel it is necessary to do so.

I wish to share with you my story of self-enlightenment in the hope that it may be of some help to you.

Before doing so I wish to explain to you how life is for me now, living as I do in this existence. I have reached a stage, a level of growth you could say, where earthly matters fade from my memory. I understand that you may not totally understand this, but in time you will as, one day, you too will move away from earthly life. One way of describing this could be to say to you to think back to a holiday that you had, let us say ten years ago. Now try and describe the holiday to me exactly in detail. You would be able to pick out the highlights, maybe even remember a few people by name if they made a big enough impression on you. You will perhaps remember a few of the not so good points of the holiday. This is how it is for me now. To try and tell you in great detail about one of my lives on earth would be virtually impossible. There is a process that we go through here that helps us recall a lifetime in order to learn from it and heal. Once learnt, however, the memories then fade, for it serves no purpose to 'live in the past'.

I hope I have explained this clearly. Having done so, I will try to hold a focus long enough to describe to you one of my lives as a Tibetan monk.

The time is 1642. I am a monk named Tai Ling, aged 22, and I am very young in many ways. I live in a beautiful monastery in a remote part of Tibet. We live very simple, humble lives, 'nothing to write home about', as you would say! A typical day for me would be one spent in prayer, meditation and tending to the crops that we lovingly grow. I have been taught in a very strict and yet loving way and it suits me fine.

I was taught to honour all life. We had very little in the way of external tools, so we would often use our hands when tending to the crops. I became very self-reliant and self-sufficient, which helped to strengthen my soul. I felt very connected to the earth and to my own connection with all of life. I grew to live more and more in harmony with the earth.

As I matured I would often go walking and would sit among the fruit trees in my favourite place to contemplate life. I would often receive visions.

I wish to share with you one of my visions, for I feel it may be relevant to many on earth.

One day, while sitting under my favourite tree contemplating life, I found myself looking at a mountain. To my astonishment a vast amount of people were climbing up the side of the mountain. What surprised me further was to see the large amount of baggage that the people carried with them. Now let me tell you that this mountain was very high and very hard going, yet the people kept on going, even though they would often fall over and cry out in pain. They were determined to reach the summit at any cost. It seemed absurd the amount of baggage they were trying to carry. Couldn't they see that if they let go of their baggage, their journey would be much easier in the long run? Onward they struggled until some finally reached the top of the mountain. I watched silently as they looked about them, worn out from their efforts, still carrying their baggage. Of course they realised that even though they had put so much effort into climbing to the top, they had not achieved what they had intended to achieve: enlightenment.

I was told to just sit and observe them quietly. I learned that large amounts of activity in one's life doesn't necessarily mean large steps forward on the path to enlightenment. Remember the story of the tortoise and the hare? You may make greater steps by just being, sitting 'under your fruit tree' and observing life, also thereby conserving energy! A releasing of their internal baggage would have made the journey much lighter for these people!

Make of this story what you will. I observe, as I

watch you from my position in life, much activity which often leads you from yourself. I acknowledge that society has made it very difficult for you to just 'sit under your tree', but try not to buy into and become engulfed by that society; be the observer. There is no need for you to go and search for a mountain to climb in order to find yourself. Do not follow the shadows of others. A wise man would let the wisdom come to him, not go searching for it. It is not necessary to struggle. Relax and allow the correct order of things to unfold in divine time.

I reached enlightenment leading a very humble life. I certainly didn't make a very big mark or impression in the world from the life that I led, for I spent a great deal of time observing from under my tree. Although my life was humble, it served me well and I made enough progress in it to reach greater heights now. To be still and observe all that is around you can teach you far more than you may think. You can learn so much from nature if only you would take the time to look and study it. Man has lost the ability to use his senses fully. It is very difficult to develop your senses surrounded by man-made material possessions. If you wish to develop your senses then I would suggest that you spend plenty of time in nature, though not rock-climbing! Just sit in silence, observe, watch, listen and above all feel.

What messages are being given to you? Did you know you have a map of your life all around you? You just need to learn how to read the map. Many of you think that you are unable to 'hear your own guidance' and so you seek it from another. Dear friends, your own personal reading is all around you!

Many live their lives with closed eyes and deaf ears, they do not see or hear what is in front of them. I call these messages 'whispers from spirit'. As you do not acknowledge these 'whispers', sometimes spirit has to shout very loud to get your attention! When this occurs, things seem to go wrong for you: perhaps your car breaks down, or the electricity fails in your home or perhaps you become ill. If you wish to avoid these extremes and live a life that is one of balance and harmony, then I suggest that you begin to read the signs given to you, begin to live your life consciously rather than unconsciously.

Many people 'go through the motions' each day, but their minds are elsewhere. Be in the know – see what lies in front of you!

There are never any coincidences. Once you understand this concept you can then begin to 'read your life'

As you walk down your busy streets, take note of advertisements on the walls and on your buses. These often give very clear statements and directions for you. Look at car registration numbers, signposts. Listen to music that is being played as a car passes you by, hear the message in the music. Look at the animals that cross your path - animals are very good messengers. When books fall off shelves, pick them up and read the open page.

Find your messages in a relaxed way, just allow spirit to let your eyes rest upon something. To go searching is defeating the object, for you once again are trying to climb mountains!

Look for the warning signs around you so that you will not need your car to be mended, or your house to be rewired. When your body is tired, rest it; then your body will not need mending either.

Cars are very good indicators of what is happening in your life. You will find that if emotions are running high, you will have water problems in your car and even in your home. Fuel problems can be telling you to look at where you are directing your energy.

There are many ways for spirit to contact you.

Sit and observe, take time to watch nature. If you look hard enough you will find it even at the heart of your large cities!

And so, my friends, stay humble, make peace with yourselves. Do not strive to be more than you are. Be content with your lives and who you are now. By doing so you will automatically enrich your lives.

I hope that my little input will have made a large impact upon you! Perhaps we will all meet one day. Until then, I wish you love and peace in your lives. A fond farewell from your brother,

Tai Ling.

Chapter 5

Working in Trust

Reflection:
'Trust in life's magical river - go with the flow!'

We are here, once again we return to you in love. Trusting in one's own abilities is not easy for some: we know this, as we are also observers! We understand that there seems to be a built-in 'self-destruct mechanism' within many. You continually 'self-destruct' any dreams that you and even others may have. This is through lack of confidence and low self-worth. You almost talk yourselves into failing before you've begun. If you could understand that love is the most powerful energy there is - for God is love - then you would know that through the power of love you could achieve anything.

Love your dreams into reality.

Creating a desirable reality to live in is not at all difficult, but for some reason you find it much easier to create hardship and turmoil for yourselves! Why? we wonder. Perhaps you enjoy living in this very limited way. We feel that you have lost the confidence in self to create desirable lives for yourselves. We cannot believe that you can enjoy living in turmoil.

The more you let go of fear-based prophecy and trust your own instincts, the easier it will become for you. You will know if you are on the right track, for life will flow. It is only when you struggle against the flow that life becomes difficult. Let go, allow yourselves to be carried along on life's magical river.

In the not-so-distant future, you will have to rely on yourselves. This is not to say that you will ever be left alone, for we shall always be there for you. However, there will come a point in your own development, when you will be asked to stand alone and walk your own path. You may lose friends along the way, for there is a tendency to isolate those who do not conform. But, my friends, you are not on the earth plane to collect as many friends as you can. Find your heart centre, your place of peace, and find the answers to all of your questions. Your guidance may well be different from that of others. Trust that your guidance is correct for you. Each man walks a different path in order to experience different outcomes. No two human paths are alike. You are individual rays of God expressing different aspects and collecting different data.

You are asked to surrender many times along your path, surrender the lower self in favour of the higher self. To surrender in favour of the higher self can be likened to letting go and floating downstream instead of clinging onto the side, frightened to let go. It takes great trust to let go and let God, we realise this. We will help you all we can but understand that fundamentally it is you who must have the courage initially to let go and trust. Trust that you will be carried along by the flow.

It is time to take your full power, not give it away to anyone. Trust that your inner voice is correct for you, even if everyone else seems to be flowing down another stream!

We also note that at times it may be difficult to trust those 'voices in your head'. You often feel it would be better if perhaps we could manifest in front of you. You feel you could trust the information given to you then. This indeed might be easier for you but it would also take your power away from you. You are learning to develop your abilities and to manifest ourselves to you would serve little purpose. You have to learn to trust in self.

Remember, the more you trust in self the more the radiance of self can shine forth. With this in mind – go and glow!

CHAPTER 6

THE CHANGING TIMES

Reflection:
'Change yourself and heal the world.'

Change is imminent, change is inevitable. Like the rays of the sun as it first touches the earth at dawn, there is always a sense of excitement and anticipation as to what the new day will bring. We can tell you with a certain sense of relief, that you are well over the critical point in time that all of your prophets have spoken about. There is indeed a sense of anticipation in the outer realms. You would be amazed if you knew half of what takes place in the outer realms - the singing of the angelic host is almost deafening! You see, we do have a sense of humour! We realise that we have been quite firm with you and even blunt at times, but we know that many of you appreciate our direct approach. As we have said, we are not here to 'mollycoddle' you into a false sense of security. We are here to prod you a little, to help you to stay awake and to help you to stay focused.

Your times are changing, and quicker than you may think. Energy is forming like a giant wave ready to carry you onto your next level of existence. There is a tendency on earth to embrace a 'I'll not believe it until I see it' attitude. We are asking you to *feel* it. There is a lot happening that you will not physically see. We tell you now that if you could see all that is occurring around you, you would be in for a big surprise! Energetically speaking, the changes are immense.

As you move further and further into the new millennium, you will find yourselves having to let go and trust more and more. All of your weaknesses will come to the surface and be revealed. Try to just go with the flow as much as you are able. The more you resist change, the harder life will get. We do not mean to alarm you, but we do want to emphasise to you that it will not serve you to try and 'cling onto the edge of the cliff'. Let go, dear friends. Know that your trust and your belief will gently carry you to the bottom of the cliff.

You may find yourselves in all sorts of situations. Many of you will be letting go of a great deal of comfort and security, though not because you have done anything wrong, dear friends: quite the opposite, we would say. In fact, you could look at it as a blessing, for in truth you are being drawn nearer and nearer to God. You are making your lives less cluttered for more service. We are not talking here about making yourselves bankrupt, to live in poverty. You can still live abundantly, although abundance doesn't necessarily always have to mean owning lots of things. If there is a need for you to travel somewhere it would be much easier with fewer attachments. We know it is often difficult for you to let go of your securities, whatever form they may take, dearest friends. Know that you are truly blessed and very much loved for your courage.

Try to stay in your heart centres through these times of change. Do not allow yourselves to go into fear: feel the fear, understand it and then move through it. You will find it becomes more and more impossible to make plans. The changing times are pushing you to go with the flow and to live in the moment, for in truth there is only *now*. There does not exist another moment. Time is an illusion. Time, as you know, is running out. This does not mean that your world is about to end. Your world, as you have known it is ending, but it is to be replaced by a much lighter, higher-frequency world, much more beautiful to behold. A much more caring society will emerge.

We have told you that there is only *now* and this is a truth, you will come to understand and know to be so. Understand that you hold all of your power in the *now*, therefore do not project your energy constantly into the 'future'. In the *now* where you exist you have the ability and the energy to create a better reality for yourselves. You certainly are not helpless in any way. You are mighty and powerful beings. In the 'past' Gods have been made Gods because they were seen to have greater powers and abilities than you and so they were put up onto pedestals and worshipped. Those days are over. You need not worship anything or any being. We feel that the reasons that you did so in the past are not relevant to speak of, for we wish to hold your focus in the now. In these changing times it is important that you learn to create your own reality. Your energy levels have been worked upon. Many of you have also been working upon yourselves to the extent that you are no longer depleting your energy levels but are instead increasing them rapidly. It would be true to say that a short while ago you would have been perhaps trying to create a mansion when you only had enough energy to create a shed! But times are changing. We would say to you that for many people this is your next step, to begin creating your reality instead of just 'bumbling along'. Start to take control of your lives in a positive way. With the energy that you all have in the *now*, decide how you wish your lives to be. Hold a focus. Direct love into that focus and say, 'My will to create'.

Dearest friends, we understand that this may send doubts into your minds. We know that you have a great deal of old patterning lodged in you and you may be fooled into thinking that it can't possibly be as simple as that! Well, we tell you with the utmost sincerity that it *is* that simple. There is nothing to it. You all do it every day unconsciously. All we are asking is that you begin to work consciously at creating a brighter future. Believe that you can do this, dear friends. The beings in your past that you thought of as Gods were no greater than you. You only believed this to be so. We have seen many times how well you create with your prayers and good intent for others and for the planet. Indeed, you have stopped many 'disasters' from occurring with your thoughts. Well, how about creating for yourselves? You deserve to live happy lives. It is your right and indeed your duty to yourselves.

You know that you create your own disease. Neither God nor anyone else gives you disease as a punishment. You are loved so much by God that your creations are allowed to unfold as you wish them to. Once again, it is old patterning that has made you believe that you should suffer in any way. Some of you believe that to be on earth means to suffer. We wish to put a stop to these belief systems straight away, for they hold you in fear and limitation. To be on the earth plane is a rare and unique privilege. You will never experience anywhere else all that you can experience on earth. There is so much that can be learnt. Just to be able to physically walk on grass is indeed a rare treat that many beings would love to experience, and yet you take it all for granted. The opportunities that are available for soul expansion on earth are breathtaking.

Dearest friends, you are not being punished, God is very benevolent. Do not become trapped with thought processes that would have you believe otherwise. It is also a 'cop out' to believe that you must suffer illness of any sort. Learn what there is to learn from the illness, then release it. There is no need to continue the illness. Some feel that they are teaching others through illness. Well, to some extent this is true, but you would teach more by showing the world how to release illness. It is a little like God asking you to reach into a fire to save a woodlouse on a burning log, you saving it and then leaving your hand in the fire to continue burning! God would not wish this for it is the act of a martyr. Put your hand in the fire, do what has to be done and then take your hand out. Allow the healing process.

Many people, we note, seem to think that it is a charitable act to be a martyr. We tell you now, it is nothing but foolhardy. It will lead you nowhere for you yourself will become another needing to be helped. Again it is the 'water well syndrome' - jumping in to 'save' someone. Help by being an example. You may not make yourself popular, as we have said before. We remind you that you are not on the earth plane to accumulate as many friends as possible. Sometimes the truth can make you very unpopular. People do not always like to hear the truth for it can shake their belief systems.

So, we will leave you for today. We would advise that you put this book down and begin to consciously CREATE! CREATE! CREATE! Let magic enter your lives! It is great fun to see your creations take form in front of your eyes. Thoughts do take form. You are a thought, the tree outside your house is a thought. All of creation started as a thought! Do you not see now how powerful thought can be?

CHAPTER 7

THE LOVE OF THE DIVINE

Reflection:
'Those with love shall become the beloved.'

We are back once more to share some home truths with you. Once again it is our pleasure to do so. We love your energy. We love everything about you. We find it difficult to understand how many people can have such little love of self. To us you are beautiful beyond belief! We love to observe your energy patterns, though we do not always love your thought patterns. We also observe with some sadness that man is often without love for his brothers and sisters. In our society we all care greatly for each other. We understand that only in so doing can we ever progress onwards into the eternal light and love of our creator. We were not always so caring. This is true. But 'time' has helped us heal our 'past' and in only so doing were we able to become an ascended civilisation.

We wish to share with you our ascension in the hope that it will help you with yours. 'Time' as we knew it (which we have to say was very different from how you view time) began to speed up. We learnt to spend a lot of time in a deep state of meditation for this helped us to stay in focus and in touch with our creator. We began to go deeply within ourselves. We understood what was happening and so it was a little easier for us. You could say we were open to it, which many of you on earth are not. This makes it more difficult for those on earth who continue to keep their eyes firmly shut to change.

Our shape and form began to become much stronger. This is occurring on earth now, we notice, and we find it quite amusing to observe your reactions to it! Understand that your bodies are becoming healthier, although some of you will have a reaction to the changes that may seem to be less than healthy. We say to you that in these cases there was a need to transmute a great deal in a short span of 'time'.

We were already very connected and open to visions and guidance. You will find that this will be something new to many of you.

Our homeland went through some changes, this is true. But not to the extent that yours is doing, and will continue to do, for we had not shown the same abuse that man has.

Understand that the ascension process is a natural occurrence. There is nothing to fear from it. It is your birthright! We view our ascension as a beautiful process and one that we are very grateful for. Ascension is a very personal thing, although it is a coming together in many ways. A coming together of self and a coming together of a nation. Remember that as within, so without. What happens within will be mirrored external to self.

God created a heaven. It was man that created a hell. Hell does not exist, at least not as you imagine it to be. Your world has to be 'cleaned up' so that it may be returned to a state of 'heaven' once more. Once it is 'clean', man will not be allowed to show such abuse again.

We have observed many people speak of returning home. There is no path to walk home. You *are* home. Stop trying to make excuses as to why you are not home within yourselves. As our dear friend Tai Ling said earlier, 'There is not the need for you to go and search for a mountain to climb in order to find yourself' - the self was never lost.

In the final days of your ascension you will find yourselves becoming very tired, having to rest and sleep more and then experiencing great rushes of energy unlike you've ever encountered before. Try to stay balanced and do not judge yourselves if you become emotional in any way. Allow yourselves to just *be*. You will also notice that you will have to live in the now. You will be unable to make plans for the 'future'. As we have said there is only *now*. This may take a little adjusting to, for we note that in your society you feel secure in your 'plan-making'. Try to let go and let God.

We welcome you, our neighbours, our brothers and sisters. We welcome your ascension.

It is the love of the divine that allows you to take this great step forward. We hope that by now you will be feeling this love that surrounds you, that blows in around you like a gentle breeze. This gentle breeze will be increasing in power. You have heard of the 'in breath' and the 'out breath' of God? Well, dear friends, you are experiencing the 'in breath,'; the breathing in of all creation, so that creation may live in harmony

49

and peace.

You are very valuable. All that you have experienced is stored within you to be recalled and learnt from. Many will learn from your time on a third dimensional planet. We are learning a great deal from you. We would like to share more information with you when you are ready. The day is nearing when we will be able to do so. The information that we and many ones are offering to you at this time is more in the way of comfort, to let you know that you are not alone and to let you know that you are loved. We have been very active in this field over the years and have dictated many books for you to read. We hope that they have served you well and have bought about a sense of peace.

We, as others, are in a sense a little 'limited' in the amount of information that we can bring you. Not because of your language barriers, for we are well equipped to align ourselves to your energies and use your language. It is more a case of 'non-interference' in your own development. We cannot give you too much information which would undoubtedly confuse you and interfere with your development. Each nation, each person ascends differently. We cannot tell you exactly how it will be for you for it depends greatly on many factors. Our main focus with you is to assist in a way which is non imposing, gentle and loving. We are indeed comrades, you and I, eternal brothers, children of our creator, loved totally and unconditionally.

CHAPTER 8
INTERNAL MIRRORS

Reflection:
'All is a reflection of self.'

I am the ascended master El Morya. Greetings, dear friends and colleagues. I come to share my energies and some words of wisdom with you. You will find my approach very direct for I am very focused. I wish to lead you out of your false sense of security that many people have built and have become trapped in.

How does one become pure unconditional love? You cannot until you have dealt with that which still remains within you. Many of you have such low self-esteem that you will never be able to love others unconditionally until you can love yourselves in this way. Work on your self-esteem, not externally but internally. You will never truly find self esteem through money or reputation, these are not solid. Always look within. You will know what needs to be addressed by your thought patterns. When you think of others do you bear any anger, resentment or jealousy? Do you still feel hurt about any situations from the past? If your answer to any of these questions is yes, then look at each issue in turn and work on it from within. 'Clean out your cupboards' until they are empty, then love will fill that space. Look at the fear that surrounds these issues. What is the worst that could possibly happen? And if it did happen would it be so bad anyway? Are your fears warranted?

Many of you fear losing people. I say to you that when you have dealt with your issues within, you will view life very differently. You will find a wholeness that you have never experienced before and you will truly find that you will not need anyone. Friends and partnerships are a bonus but not a necessity to your happiness.

Life is a mirror of your own creations. If you truly understand this concept then you will understand that only by going within, pulling out all of your skeletons from the cupboards, talking yourself through these issues, seeing where they first gave birth and then lovingly releasing them, only then can you love outside of self unconditionally.

How many of you dear souls can truly say that you are unaffected by others' criticisms? How many of you can truly say that you never enter into a good gossip about someone? Why do you think you do this? Because you have not learnt unconditional love. I realise that life on earth is not easy. I too had to learn the same lessons that you are learning, so it can be done!

Imagine life on earth to be like entering a giant maze, only the hedges or walls are made out of mirrors. You are given a few clues at the beginning and then the rest is up to you. How far do you honestly think you will get? Many people become stuck quite early on, staring at a mirror image of themselves that is a false illusion.

Some may go a little further, facing the dark images that look back at them, facing them and moving on. Some find themselves going round and round in circles, constantly repeating old patterns. If you were to stop and look into the mirror now, what image would present itself to you? What reality have you created? What would reflect back to you? Perhaps a few worry lines, a few stress wrinkles? You know, in truth, you do not need to age, dear friends. When you love yourself unconditionally you can stay looking youthful.

You will not find an ascended master with stress lines on his or her face. We have had to master self-esteem in order to become masters of our reality. Many of you are not in control of your reality. You just let life throw at you what it will. You struggle on through, muddling along, never really achieving what you wish to achieve. You use excuses to justify your situation – 'I am in this situation to teach someone a lesson'. I say to you that this way of thinking will not help anyone. You are not teaching anyone anything useful. These are the words of a martyr. You are taking the easy route, giving in, putting up with situations because you find it easier to do so than to take charge of your life and change its course. And so you will justify your lethargy by telling everyone, thus convincing yourself, that you are in service, on a mission to 'save the world'. Well, my friend, it is you who needs to be saved.

Again, any situation that you find yourself in is an outward reflection of your inner state of beingness. I tell you now, dear friends, that no one will give you a pat on the back for 'staying behind', sacrificing yourself to others and thus staying at their levels of growth. Be strong, take control, let others follow if they wish. Do not feel it is your duty to pull them along.

We who are masters of our reality do not experience pain in our bodies. We do not have any resistance to change. We do not have fear, we have seen the illusion. We do not have worry frowns and lines. We live in peace and in love for we create it to be so. We can 'manipulate' energy, will energy into beingness because we have first looked within. You will be able to do the same once you stop hiding your past, keeping it buried deep within because it is easier to do so than release it. Yes, you may well feel a little battered and scarred from all the clearing, but your scars will heal, my friends. Your tears will eventually dry and a radiance will be seen glowing around you.

Beloveds, I humbly ask you to accept these words in love. The path to self mastery is not an easy one. It is an inner adventure filled with wonder and surprise. You are like Alice in Wonderland! You may not always like what you find hidden deep within you. Persevere, dear friends. I look forward to greeting you all warmly one day, thank you for taking the time to be with me. I salute you in love,

El Morya.

CHAPTER 9
THE CARETAKERS

Reflection:
'As the Father, as the son...'

Good day, dear ones, we greet you in love. We wish to talk this day about your responsibilities as parents. Those of you who are already parents will know of the great responsibility that is in your hands, for you are raising the next generation. Great care must be made not to raise them with the 'old patterning' that you had and are trying to clear. They should be raised with love and respect for all of life.

We note that in your society you are appalled when you hear of a murder. Yet you are all murderers in a sense, for you regularly kill the dreams of those around you, particularly those that you claim to love. You tell them that they are unable to attend further education because they are not bright enough. You tell them that they will never make a model for they are not pretty enough. They are not talented enough, too fat, too thin etc. You say that you are only trying to protect them from getting hurt. We say that you are denying their right to learn. This 'protecting' method can actually do far more harm than good, for you kill their

55

dreams and this form of murder is very long-lasting. It becomes engraved in a child very deeply, causing future feelings of unworthiness. You all know of these feelings for many of you have the same 'problem', probably caused by the same method of 'love'.

Encourage your children, even if they wish to do something which you feel is way out of their capabilities. Don't deny them the experience of learning for themselves. Let them grow and explore all of their potentiality. Encourage them to explore themselves, to develop into confident beings. Yes, we dare say that there will be times when they will be hurt, but earth life is for learning. Let them learn in their own way, of their own choosing.

In the future earth schools will be very different. We are not altogether in favour of your school training now. It seems very limiting. Children often emerge from school life with very little knowledge about matters of most importance. Quite often they emerge with the 'stuffing totally knocked out of them', with very little in the way of self-worth. We would recommend that you 'shop around' for a good spiritually-based school. In the future these will not be so few and far between. Look for schools which encourage learning in a more natural sense.

In our society children are raised with the utmost care and attention. They are supported and nurtured and a great deal of time and care is spent teaching them about the web of life, the intricacies of energy patterns, Universal laws and cosmic relations. We pride ourselves on our children.

A great deal is involved in choosing parenthood in our society. We take into consideration a great many factors. We do not produce offspring to 'make us complete', as many on earth do. It is quite common amongst you to get married, still not be satisfied and so have children to fulfil your own needs. Invariably people discover that they are still not satisfied, still not complete. Of course you will never find what you are looking for outside of self. We mention this throughout this book so that we can make this point to you in many different ways, but always returning to this truth. You can marry, divorce, remarry, have lots of children, maybe a new car every year to park in the garage - better still, to park outside of the house so that all your neighbours can see how well you are doing! You can accumulate as many possessions as you wish, but we tell you now, you will never find true peace, wholeness and oneness in your life through these means.

There are many souls who are 'queuing up' to be born into these momentous times. In a sense the children that are being born into the earth plane now are indeed 'special souls'. We hesitate to speak of 'special souls', for understand that *all* souls are equal. It would be better and more correct to say 'different souls'.

'Old souls' have re-entered into the earth plane many, many times before, re-learning many, many lessons, climbing their way steadily up life's long and somewhat weary ladder. This method of learning on this plane is coming to an end. There will be other 'schools' to train in with equal learning opportunities. This planet is about to advance beyond your current comprehension. These 'old souls' who remain on this plane will have evolved enough to stay here physically.

The 'new souls' coming in are already evolved to this point. They do not need to undergo the same learning process that you have undergone. They are well equipped to deal with earth's lessons, they have all the tools. Because their vibration is much finer and their bodies less dense, they will not experience lower vibrational experiences. Let us say that they have not come to the earth plane to experience illness, pain or any other form of limitation. Their form will be slightly different from yours, maybe not visibly, but something new from within. They will have all 12 strands of DNA fully active. Therefore all of their psychic abilities will be turned on.

These children are the new starseeds on the earth plane, the next generation that will help to remove fear and doubts. They will cover the land like a vast sea of light and will grow in each country. Every dark corner will be lit by their radiance. Open your arms to these children, bless them for their presence. The birthing of a new world has truly begun.

CHAPTER 10

THE SUMMARY

Reflection:
'Reflections from the book.'

It is true to say that God is everywhere. How could it not be so, for there is only one spirit and that spirit is God. Spirit is everywhere: and you cannot escape God, although you can ignore God. Burying yourself in the material world will not cut yourself off. You cannot be cut off from God. How could you, God is everywhere and in all things, including you! All that you can do is close your eyes, but it will not make God disappear.

'Making your way back to God' is just a case of putting a 'welcome' mat outside your front door! You may wish to clean up your 'house' first, clear away the clutter, weed the garden, throw away the baggage, clear away the cobwebs of the past and invariably make your house more inviting!

We are being humorous here, although it is true to say that you will be asked to 'empty thy house and weed thy garden' to allow only that which is pure to grow there.

Those of you with many material possessions may

need a little convincing, however! Of course it is not wrong to own a nice car, house or boat, but don't let them become your one focus. Love God with all your might and the rest will follow. You have heard the saying 'You can't take it with you when you go!' Well, this is true of material possessions. Once you have found eternal peace you would never wish for anything else, for nothing could match the peace and love that you will feel within God's embrace.

We wish to remind you that your world was created in love. You are created in love. You were birthed by love into love. God created you. God is love, everything is love. With this in mind we hope that you will have more respect for all life on your planet.

If you truly understand this concept of oneness that we have passed onto you, you will understand that each time you judge another in any way, you are passing judgement on God's creation, God's love. You are making a statement that God's love isn't good enough, but is flawed and imperfect. Each time that you look at yourself in a mirror and criticise your looks, you criticise God's love. Whenever you complain that you are not 'spiritually connected enough, open enough, aligned enough' or anything else that you may complain about, again you question God's love. It is because of God - love- that you are. Know that God is in all things: the air that you breathe, the water you drink and bathe in, the food that nourishes your bodies. How could you possibly feel alone? Aloneness comes through closed eyes and deaf ears.

There is no end to life, life is eternal. Why should God create anything in love that does not last eternally? God loves what is created. You were created in that same love, therefore you are eternal. You do not and cannot die. You will evolve, mature, develop and grow more and more in God's love.

Know that fear exists where love doesn't. When you enter the heart centre, fear cannot exist. When you experience fear know that you have stepped out of love. Only that of love is truth, all else is illusory. Try to see which fears are warranted and which are illusory. When you look at your fears you will see that none of them hold any firm ground, so don't create them to be so.

Look at that which you fear and send love to the fear. Dissolve it in love. You will then see it disappear. Stop creating more fear patterns. Do not recreate or create new fears into your life. Do not become a martyr to fear, you are not helping anyone. If you are surrounded by fearful situations and fearful people we would suggest that you look at your own fears first. Do not be misled into thinking it is your work on the earth plane to be with fearful people, even if you believe you are helping them. Heal thyself and all will be healed. Remove fear from your life and fear will not exist. It only exists where it has fertile ground. Do not stay and continually water this ground. Know that the fearful will create fearful events and fearful people into their lives. Decide if that's the life for you. If not, begin creating the sort of life that you do wish to experience.

Learn to work with energy. Mould energy like clay, so that it becomes real and usable. It is a time to focus on your goals in life, that which you wish to achieve. Keep focusing on them, pull them into your reality.

Any great master who has walked the earth plane did not become a master without first learning how to work with energy.

Try to justify all that you do in love. If you cannot then don't do it. Follow your heart at all times. Do not be persuaded by others to follow their dreams, theirs may be the totally wrong direction for you. If it doesn't *feel* right then it is wrong for you.

Remember, those who stand in judgement shall attract the judgmental and be judged themselves. Those who stand for greed shall attract the greedy. Those who stand for freedom shall attract the free and be set free. Those who stand for truth shall attract truth and become enlightened. Those who stand for love shall stand in love and become the beloved.

This is Universal Law.

God bless.